Sports Illustrated
HANDBALL

The Sports Illustrated Library

BOOKS ON TEAM SPORTS

Baseball	Football: Defense	Ice Hockey
Basketball	Football: Offense	Soccer
Curling: Techniques and Strategy	Football: Quarterback	Volleyball

BOOKS ON INDIVIDUAL SPORTS

Badminton	Horseback Riding	Table Tennis
Fly Fishing	Judo	Tennis
Golf	Skiing	Track: Running Events
Handball	Squash	

BOOKS ON WATER SPORTS

Powerboating	Small Boat Sailing
Skin Diving and Snorkeling	Swimming and Diving

SPECIAL BOOKS

Dog Training	Training with Weights
Safe Driving	

Sports Illustrated
HANDBALL

By WAYNE J. McFARLAND
and PHILIP SMITH

Illustrations
by Frank Mullins

J. B. LIPPINCOTT COMPANY
Philadelphia and New York

Cover photograph: Heinz Kluetmeier
Photograph on page 8: Roy DeCarava
Photograph on page 45: Herb Scharfman
Photograph on page 95: Arthur Shay

U.S. Library of Congress Cataloging in Publication Data

McFarland, Wayne J
Sports illustrated handball.

(The Sports illustrated library)
Includes index.
1. Handball. I. Smith, Philip, birth date
joint author. II. Mullins, Frank. III. Sports
illustrated (Chicago). IV. Title.
GV1017.H2M2   796.31   75–28486
ISBN–0–397–01095–8
ISBN–0–397–01106–7 (pbk.)

Contents

Sports Illustrated
HANDBALL

1
The Setting

THE OLD IRISH HARDBALL GAME of handball was brought across the Atlantic Ocean to the United States during the 1800s and was the source for today's popular game of four-wall handball. Today's game is played on a smaller court and with a softer ball, but the demands placed on a player's quickness, physical conditioning, ambidexterity and ability to make lightning-fast decisions remain unchanged.

The modern four-wall court is a shoe-box-shaped area

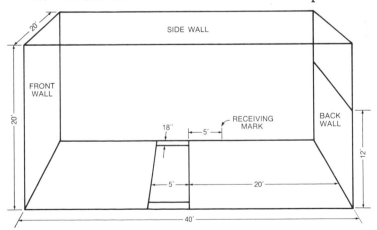

Diagram 1. Standard official dimensions of the four-wall handball court.

40 feet long, 20 feet wide and 20 feet high. The standard ball is made of black rubber; it has a diameter of about 1⅞ inches and weighs approximately 2.3 ounces. Young and old alike can send this small ball rebounding about the court at high speeds; whereas the speed of the moving ball places a premium on the quickness and strength of youth, the innumerable angles taken by the ball off walls, floor and ceiling give an edge to the wisdom and skill of the older player. Handball is truly a lifetime sport.

SPONSORSHIP

The sponsorship of four-wall handball in the United States has long been an important activity of the Young Men's Christian Association, the National Jewish Welfare Board, the Amateur Athletic Union and local organizations such as the Detroit Athletic Club. Thanks to the monies and facilities of these athletic-minded urban agencies, four-wall handball players have grown over the years in both numbers and ability. Among the present generation, Robert W. "Bob" Kendler ranks as handball's most outstanding individual. A five-time national doubles champion who also created the glass handball court, he was one of the founding fathers at the birth of the United States Handball Association in 1951.

At the college level, the USHA has conducted a national intercollegiate four-wall tournament since 1954. At a higher competitive level in the United States, four-wall handball is formally organized by the USHA into an annual series of four geographically designated divisional tournaments the champions of which compete in the United States National Senior Handball Singles and Doubles Championships. The list of recent USHA national champions clearly indicates the preeminent position attained by Paul Haber, whose feats in the court place him with the greatest players of yester-year: Bill "Murderball" Ranft, the first national singles champion (1919); Joe "Blonde Panther" Platak, winner of seven consecutive national singles titles (1935–41); Vic Hershkowitz, considered by many the best all-around performer ever; and Jimmy Jacobs, whose performances while winning six national singles and six national doubles four-wall titles vividly demonstrated the importance of spartan conditioning and intelligent tactics. Many players classify Jimmy as probably the greatest of all four-wall champions.

During the winter of 1973–74 professional handball became a reality for players in the United States, with Fred Lewis winning top honors for the five-tournament tour sponsored and sanctioned by the National Handball Club. In April 1975 the second year of professional handball closed with the Las Vegas Classic, an event conducted in conjunction with the finals of USHA's twenty-fifth annual four-wall national championships.

RULES

The Unified Handball Rules were formulated in 1959. This set of thirty-five rules and their numerous subsections is the framework within which today's players—both beginners and veterans—are expected to play. It is helpful for beginners to remember that the official rules are a product of many decades of play, discussion, writing and rewriting; the best way to learn them is to start with those ideas that structure the game and then refine and add to your understanding by getting into a court and playing. The structural ideas for one-wall and three-wall handball are essentially the same as those for four-wall handball.

1. The ball may be hit with either hand, but with only one hand at a time. When the wrist, forearm or other part of a player strikes the ball, the hit is not legal.

2. A pair of gloves must be worn, the purpose of which is to prevent perspiration on the player's hands from wetting the ball.

3. The server is the player who possesses the opportunity or privilege of initiating play. A serve is any ball hit or swung at by the server in an attempt to put the ball into play.

4. A return is a ball already in play which is hit legally in an attempt to send it back to the front wall.

5. A point is a tally awarded the server or serving team; it is assigned or allowed whenever the server's opponent fails to make a legal return.

6. An out is loss of service; it is a penalty assigned to the server whenever he fails to put the ball in play or fails to make a legal return.

7. The first player or team to earn twenty-one points is the winner of a game. Match is the best two out of three games.

8. A player or team can score points only when in possession of service. A server continues to serve until an out is earned; theoretically, a player or team could win 21–0.

9. To remain in play, every ball legally hit must legally reach the front wall before touching the floor. A serve must travel directly from the server's hand to the front wall. A return may touch the walls or ceiling any number of times before touching the front wall.

10. Every ball that legally touches the floor must be hit again before it touches the floor a second time; failure to strike such a ball on the first hop earns either an out or a point.

11. In games or matches having no assigned referee, a hinder may be called to indicate that the opponent interfered with you or with the ball. A hinder is called by shouting, "Hinder!" Such a call immediately stops play, thus providing time for the person who shouted to explain why he thinks a hinder occurred. The opponent may or may not agree with the call, for sometimes the opponent's judgment of what happened during the furious swiftness of handball differs from the judgment of the person making the call. At such times, goodwill is the only real basis for

settlement, and the most frequently selected solution is re-play of the volley. When an assigned referee declares a hinder, he orders the volley replayed if he judges the inter-ference to have been unavoidable, and rules either an out or a point if he deems the interference to have been avoidable.

CENTER-COURT TERRITORY

The most valuable real estate in handball is center-court territory, an imaginary circular area approximately 6 feet in diameter that, strange as it may seem, is not in the true center of the court. The center point of this make-believe circle is equidistant from each side wall but about 3 feet closer to the back wall than to the front wall. This ad-

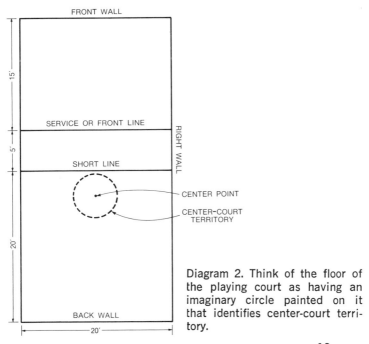

Diagram 2. Think of the floor of the playing court as having an imaginary circle painted on it that identifies center-court terri-tory.

13

justment of three feet off true center is made because (1) it is easier for most players to move forward than it is for them to move backward; and (2) in most games there are fewer returns that force the players into the front half of the court than there are returns that can best be stroked from the back half of the playing area.

Beginners should position themselves at the center point of center-court territory. This is not always possible, of course, for three reasons: (1) the opponent may already be in this location; (2) the action is fast and changing, and center point is difficult to locate under such conditions; and (3) the ball may be located so far from center court that the player must leave or avoid this territory in order to execute the stroke successfully. Nevertheless, beginners should become conscious of center court and always strive to position themselves there. Center point of this territory is merely a guidepost; during a game the player seldom occupies this point, but he should be in the territory often.

Being in center-court territory is important because it places you in the best possible location from which to reach three types of shots—shots that, when performed successfully by your opponent, force you to move outside the area. These are (1) a kill shot, which by definition hits exceedingly close to the bottom of the front wall; (2) the kind of lob shot that travels over your head and touches the floor near the back wall; (3) the kind of pass shot that is close to a side wall and parallel to it until entering backcourt territory.

SERVICE ZONE

Unlike center-court territory, the service zone is clearly defined by painted lines and playing regulations. The painted line closest to the front wall is officially named the service line, but most veteran players speak of it as the front line. This line, 1½ inches in width, is parallel to and 15 feet from the front wall. Parallel to the service or front line at a distance of 20 feet from the front wall is the short line, so named because one of the requirements of a legal serve is that it must travel beyond this line before touching the floor; any serve that fails to do so is classified as short. During the excitement and rush of competitive play the short line may be helpful in locating center-court territory, since it divides the court into equal front and back areas.

There are two service boxes within the service zone. These are needed only for doubles play; when playing singles, you should pretend that these service boxes do not exist. In doubles, the server's partner is expected to stand erect with his back to the side wall until the serve passes

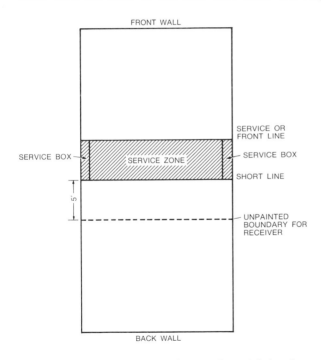

Diagram 3. The ball must be put into play from the service zone.

the short line; he is also required to have both feet on the floor within the service box.

All servers in handball, as in tennis, are allowed two attempts at putting the ball into play. A server may stand anywhere he chooses within the service zone and deliver his serve from this selected location. The lines painted on the floor to designate the service zone are a part of this territory, and the server's shoe may touch any part of these lines without penalty. However, if any part of a shoe extends past either the service line or the short line before the serve legally rebounds over the short line, a foot fault has occurred, and the serve is called a short. The penalty for executing any short is loss of one service attempt. Any two consecutive shorts earn an out.

SPECTATORS

The Unified Handball Rules require that the back wall be "at least 12 feet high"; this wording allows the back wall to be shorter than the front, thus permitting a small gallery for spectators, and for a referee if one is assigned to the match.

It is the use of glass, however, that has made it possible to showcase handball in a manner unknown to and unimagined by players of earlier decades. Glass side and back walls allow more than one thousand spectators at a time to share the dynamics of four-wall handball.

16

2
The Hands

THE HUMAN HANDS are to the handball player as the racket is to the tennis player, so your hands deserve the same loving care. Whether you are a beginning player or a seasoned veteran of many years, there are many ways to condition your hands so they perform at top efficiency.

HAND CARE

Before playing, you should warm up your hands so that an increased supply of blood reaches all the muscles, tendons and tissues used in striking the ball. A convenient and easy first step in this warm-up is to massage your hands as you walk from the locker room to the court. If you have time, try soaking your hands in warm or hot water for a couple of minutes. As a good protective procedure, you may also wrap white, perforated, lightweight adhesive tape across the upper part of each palm. For this taping, use two

17

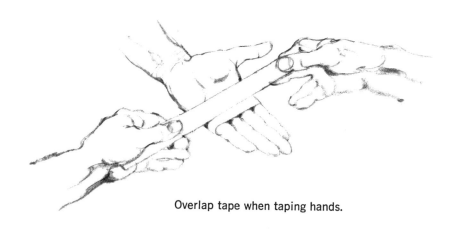

Overlap tape when taping hands.

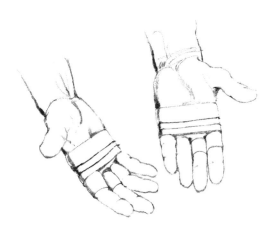

Use three pieces of tape if hands are large.

or three strips of tape, each approximately ¾ inch in width. Apply the second piece of tape over the first, covering about half of the first strip. If you have unusually large hands and need a third piece of tape, cover approximately

18

one-half of the second strip in the same manner as you covered the first strip.

SELECTING YOUR GLOVES

Many players prefer soft, thin leather gloves. This type of glove brings the hand closer to the ball and, some players believe, increases control over the ball. For a beginner, however, the gloves should be constructed of thick leather with a padded area for the palms, since the emphasis at this time is on protection of the hands at the cost of some ball control. You can get additional protection by wearing white cotton gloves under the leather gloves. Wearing these inner gloves is much like wearing two pairs of socks; that is, it reduces friction between skin and leather gloves, absorbs perspiration and reduces some of the shock upon impact with the ball. These gloves should all fit snugly. The

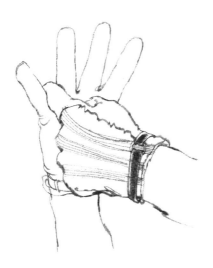

Proper glove fit.

single best indicator of a good fit is when the corresponding part of the glove snugly touches the bottom of the valley between each set of two fingers. Surprisingly, the snugness at the base of this valley is more important to top efficiency than the fit of the gloves at the fingertips.

SHAKING HANDS WITH THE BALL

Most beginners ask, "How do I hold my hand when I hit the ball?" The best answer to this question is "The way you do while shaking hands with someone."

Most people shake hands with a semirelaxed hand. In handball a hand held this way gives with the impact of the ball, thus creating a hydraulic-type action as the ball gradually slows down; if the hand is tense and taut, it does not give with the impact of the ball. Ideally, the area on the hand that contacts the ball is the base of the first two fingers and adjoining portions of the palm.

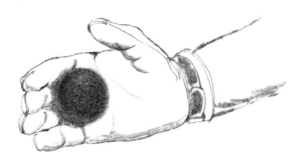

Proper hand position.

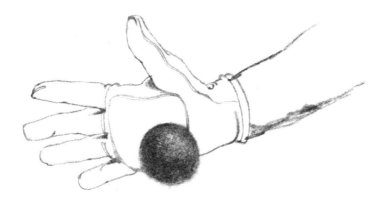

Hand tense, taut (wrong).

When you shake hands; you don't want to shake the arm off the other person. The same is true when you swing at the handball, for too hard a swing reduces your control over the ball. Only after you have developed some success in controlling the ball will you increase the velocity of your arm movement.

THE FIST

You may use your fist as well as your open hand to strike the ball. By developing skill with the fist, you will be able to apply much more power to the ball with a much lower expenditure of energy than if you used your open hand. Hitting the ball with your fist is like hitting it with a plate of lead! The resulting increase in ball speed, however, is not an unmixed blessing, for you also lose some ball control.

21

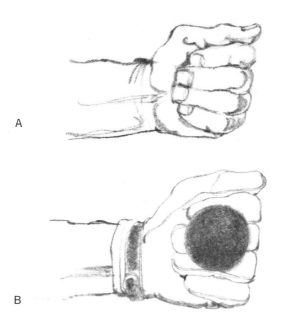

A

B

Handball fist. Press fingertips tightly onto heel of hand (A) or into the palm (B).

To form a fist, press the last segment of each finger tightly onto the heel of your hand. Place your thumb on top of the first segment of your first finger. This fist is unlike the fist formed by a boxer in that your fingernails are not buried into your palm and your thumb is not lying across several fingers. When using your hand as a fist, make contact with the ball with the back of your fingers.

PROTECTING YOUR FINGERTIPS

Handball players often injure their fingertips by hitting them against the wall. This usually occurs when a player

22

Protecting fingertips.

attempts to return the ball while it is close to or touching a wall. It is difficult to pluck the ball from such a surface, and even when a player's judgment, hand coordination and eyesight are very good, he can be injured this way.

The best way to prevent such an injury is to hold your hand with your fingers pointing up if the ball is above the waist, and with your fingers pointing down if the ball is waist high or lower. When your fingers are pointing up, the fleshy part of the side of your hand below the little finger hits the wall (much like a karate chop), and this area is less vulnerable to injury than are your fingertips. When your fingers are pointed down and your thumb is pressed against your palm, the fleshy part of the side of the hand above the forefinger is exposed instead of your fingertips.

3
Watching the Ball

WATCHING THE BALL means keeping your eye on the ball every instant. Watch it as it leaves your opponent's hand. Watch it as it strikes the front wall. Watch it as it caroms from side wall to front wall to side wall. Watch it right up to the instant your hand strikes it.

The secret of watching the ball is to position your body so that your eyes constantly have an unobstructed line of sight to the ball, and the only way to accomplish this is by perpetual footwork. For example, when a return you have hit to the front wall has touched the left wall and

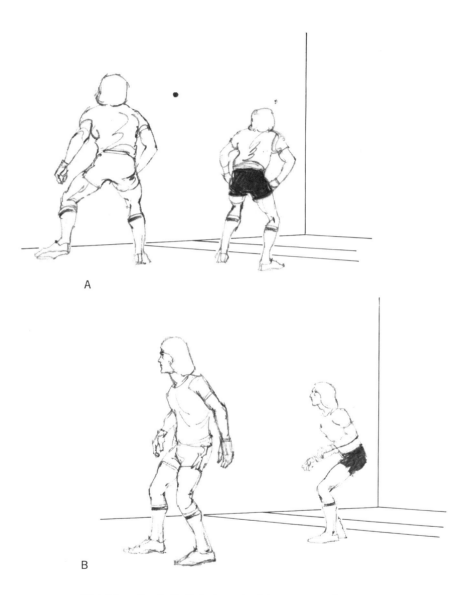

A

B

Watching the ball. It is important to turn continually to face the flight of the ball. On these two pages, note how the player in center court correctly pivots to face both the ball and his opponent.

C

D

is moving toward the middle of the back wall with your opponent in hot pursuit, you should be facing the ball and your opponent. As the ball touches the middle of the back wall, both your toes and your eyes are directed toward the back wall. As the ball moves off the back wall toward the right wall, you begin pivoting on your right foot and simultaneously move your left foot closer to both the right wall and the front wall.

PRESTROKE POSTURE

Your ability to move so that you constantly face the ball depends to a great extent on your prestroke posture. Whether you are motionless, as when waiting to receive a serve, or moving about the court in order to keep your eye on the ball, the best prestroke stance is one that permits you to move instantaneously and in any direction the swiftly flying ball demands. Ideally, your knees are bent and your weight is forward on the balls of your feet. Your

Prestroke posture.

elbows are approximately 7 to 9 inches away from your ribs; your forearms are almost horizontal to the playing floor, while your hands are open and slightly lower than your elbows. Your upper body is leaning forward from the waist, thus placing your head further forward than your toes.

THE GLIDE STEP

When used in conjunction with the proper prestroke stance, the glide step is the player's most effective method of moving from one location to another. With knees bent and feet apart, a player can pivot in either direction, shuffle forward or backward, glide to either side, jump, dive or run. In the glide step one foot is never crossed over the other, and the distance between feet is always more or less the same as the distance from shoulder to shoulder.

The glide step. The key to this step is never crossing the feet. Keep them in line with the shoulders until the swing begins.

This combination of proper posture and constant footwork enables the player to focus his eyes on the ball until he strikes it. This is vital, for if you watch the ball as your hand strikes it you cannot possibly raise your head and look away. Golfers and baseball players, among others, realize that if you look to see where the ball is going before you actually strike it, you will make an error. The same is true in handball! If you raise your head, you also raise your shoulders; and by raising your shoulders, you are moving your hand a little farther away from the ball. This changes the relationship of the ball and your hand just before you strike the ball, resulting in bad shots.

PROTECTING YOUR EYES

Most beginners, we have observed, avoid watching the ball constantly because they dislike exposing their face and eyes fully to the ball whenever they are in center-court territory and their opponent is about to hit the ball from backcourt territory. Veteran players often protect themselves successfully in this situation by holding one hand in front of their eyes, almost at arm's length, with their fingers spread apart so that they can maintain visual reference with the ball at all times. For players who do not wear glasses but are particularly concerned with eye protection, there are at least two kinds of eye-guard devices that are inexpensive and extremely effective. For those who wear glasses, metal frames and impact-resistant lenses are recommended.

4
Stroking the Ball

NEW PLAYERS seldom realize the difference between eye action during a stroke and that during a throw. When making a throw, the player holds the ball in his hand and carries it through space, grasping it in his hand all the time. He need not be concerned about the location of the ball, and his eyes are free to focus on the target. When executing a stroke in handball, however, the player must focus his eyes on a ball whose location is ever-changing and must attempt to strike this moving object with one of his hands. Thus, for a stroke the player is required to concentrate on the ball rather than the target.

Most beginners find it particularly difficult to use the "off," or nondominant, hand in striking the ball, but it is a serious mistake to avoid using this hand. Remember that the goal is to be ambidextrous, and the time to start using the off hand is sooner rather than later. An experienced handball player will discover quickly whether or not you can effectively use your off hand; if you cannot, the veteran

31

player will repeatedly select targets that force you to use your off hand, so that you will inevitably lose the game.

You must not, however, use only one hand at a time. Every stroke is simultaneously a two-handed skill, and the movement of the hand that does not strike the ball is as important as that of the hand hitting the ball. It is bad form to cradle the nonstroking arm close to the body, because an arm held in this way cannot adequately lead or influence the complicated movements that follow it, resulting in an undesirable loss in both control and power.

CLASSIC SIDEARM STROKE

In this stroke, which begins as do all strokes, your toes are pointed toward the side wall. Your knees are bent and your weight is forward on the balls of your feet so that you can move immediately in the required direction. Your elbows are approximately 7 to 9 inches away from your ribs; your forearms are almost horizontal to the playing

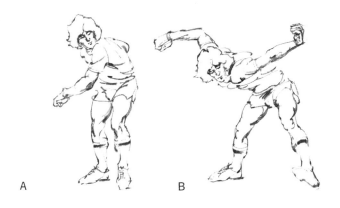

A   B

The sidearm stroke. In the windup, both arms move back and away from the approaching ball (A). During the forward swing, power is increased by flinging the front arm forward (B); the striking arm

floor, and your hands are open and slightly lower than your elbows. Your upper body is leaning forward from the waist, thus placing your head farther forward than your toes.

The classic sidearm stroke can be broken down into three parts: backswing, forward swing and follow-through.

Backswing

As the ball approaches, prepare yourself for a hit by executing the backswing or windup portion of the stroke. This windup begins simultaneously with movement in your arms, hips, knees and feet. Move your striking arm back and around slightly to the rear; your other arm follows and comes in front of the chest. At the same time shift your body weight to the back foot, move your back hip around to the rear and raise the heel of your front foot off the floor. When you are shifting your weight to the back foot, do not move your back knee in the direction of your striking arm, even though your front knee has shifted considerably in that direction.

C   D   E

is bent at the elbow (C) and the body rotates as the striking hand moves through the point of contact (D). Complete the follow-through by pointing at the side wall with your striking hand (E).

Forward Swing

You begin the forward swing from the windup position (completed backswing). Start moving your front hand, which is in line with your chest, forward and rotate your hips toward the ball. At this point your knees move toward the ball, the heel of your front foot returns to the ground as the body weight shifts forward and your striking arm is pulled along in the direction of the ball. Ideally, the elbow of the striking arm is closer to the floor than is the hand that will make contact with the ball. Just prior to contact, the lower arm and striking hand move quickly forward, with the wrist moving very quickly just before contact to provide the final impetus to the returning ball. This accelerated forward motion of the wrist is similar to the motion used by a baseball pitcher in throwing a fast ball.

Follow-through

The classic sidearm stroke ends, as do all strokes, in the follow-through. You can best learn this final stage of the stroke by reaching outward with your striking arm after

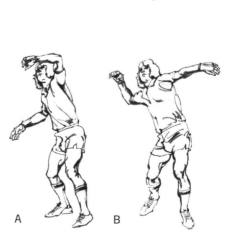

A   B

The overarm stroke. The windup begins by dropping the striking hand down and to the rear (A). The forward swing begins with the striking hand moving up, the front arm forward and down (B). The

you hit the ball, and making an imaginary touch with the fingers on the wall toward which your fingers are now pointing. The stroke is complete when your striking arm is halted because your feet, knees and hips have also stopped moving. Until this final instant, which is only a temporary position, you should have freedom of movement in each joint.

CLASSIC OVERARM STROKE

You should begin the classic overarm stroke facing the side wall, with your knees bent and your weight forward on the balls of your feet. Be sure that your elbows, forearms and hands are positioned for the prestroke stance and that your upper body is leaning forward from the waist.

Backswing

As the ball approaches, begin your backswing by moving your arms, hips, knees and feet simultaneously. Your striking arm goes back and toward the floor, and your other

C   D   E

elbow of the striking arm leads the hand through (C), the striking shoulder rotates forward (D), with the arm reaching out to complete and follow through (E).

elbow faces the approaching ball. As your striking arm continues moving into position, your other arm follows and comes into a high, sharply bent position; the elbow should be level with your forehead, your hand should be level with your nose, and the back of your hand should almost touch your nose or mouth.

Meanwhile, your back knee remains in place and your back hip also remains motionless, thus permitting you to bend at the waist in the direction your striking arm is moving. This unusual and delicate movement is vital; practice it off-court in slow motion. This shifting of your body weight draws your front knee to the rear and the heel of your front foot off the floor.

Forward Swing

The movement of your front hand is not identical to that for the sidearm stroke, where you bring it forward along a line parallel to the floor. Here you move it forward and up.

At the same time you shift your body weight forward and take a short step toward the ball with your front foot. Then move your back knee forward; this pulls your striking arm powerfully into action.

As your back knee moves forward, your elbow bends to bring the hand upward. At the same time your elbow and wrist rotate so that the palm of your hand is pointed toward the ceiling. At this moment your striking arm is positioned as it would be if you were about to throw a baseball; that is, your elbow is approximately level with your shoulder, and your hand, with the palm facing up, is slightly above the shoulder. The next move is forward and slightly up, with the elbow leading and the hand trailing. Your elbow should always be lower than the hand. Immediately before your hand makes contact with the ball, bring your forearm and striking hand forward and snap your wrist to provide the final impetus to the ball. At the moment of contact your hand leads the elbow and, ideally, is forward of and slightly higher than your forehead.

Follow-through

As in the other strokes, the follow-through is complete when you have stopped moving your striking arm and your fingers are making imaginary contact on one of the walls. You can practice the follow-through at home, without a ball, in front of a full-length mirror.

CLASSIC UNDERARM STROKE

As in the previous two strokes, your toes are pointed toward the side wall and your knees are bent, thus shifting your weight forward onto the balls of your feet. Your elbows are approximately 7 to 9 inches away from your ribs; your forearms, hands, upper body and head are positioned for the prestroke stance, from which you begin the backswing.

Backswing

Again, start the backswing by moving your arms, hips, knees and feet simultaneously. Bring your striking arm back and up until the full length of your hand is higher than your head. With your hand in this position, your elbow will be approximately level with your ear. During practice sessions you can look at this hand to check its position; if you have to look up, it is at the proper height. Only the back of your hand should be visible; the palm of your hand, at the top of the backswing, points away from the approaching ball.

Meanwhile, bring your nonstriking arm in front of your abdomen. (Note that this arm is closer to the floor than it is in the sidearm stroke.) At the same time, shift your

37

body weight to the back foot and bring your back hip slightly up and out in the direction of your striking arm. Raise the heel of your front foot off the floor and keep your back knee in place while you bend your front knee considerably in the direction taken by your striking arm.

Forward Swing

First, step forward with your front foot. Your back knee should begin to dip toward the floor and move toward the ball. This motion is essential to the stroke, as it forcefully pulls your striking arm down toward the ball and gives you extra power.

Ideally you should make contact with the ball at knee level, just as you bring your striking arm upward and forward. Your lower arm and striking hand swing forcefully forward the moment before contact, and your wrist snaps quickly in order to provide final impetus to the ball.

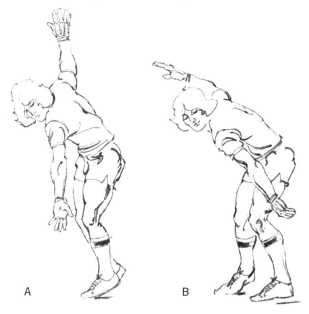

A   B

The underarm stroke. The front hand is low, near the knee (A). As the forward swing begins, the back knee begins to dip and the striking arm bends slightly (B). At contact, the striking hand

Follow-through

Again, after hitting the ball you should reach outward with your striking arm and make imaginary contact on the wall with your fingers. At the completion of the follow-through your other arm is above and behind your head.

WHERE CONTACT IS MADE

The most important moment in every stroke is contact with the ball. Watching the ball and moving your feet are merely preliminary steps to this moment; you should pay particular attention to that point in space where your striking hand or fist does indeed contact the ball. Such a point in space is more difficult for the new handball player to perceive than for his counterpart in baseball. In the game of baseball balls and strikes are called in relation to an immovable object (home plate) in order to guarantee that

C   D

is moving upward (C) and follows through extended, with the striking shoulder rotated forward (D).

most pitches will be in front of the stroker (batter). In handball, however, this sort of assistance is not available, and the player must constantly move his feet in order to get the ball in front of him. In handball, as in baseball, a late swing means that your hand struck the ball after it passed the center of your body; an early swing means that your hand struck the ball before it reached a point in space opposite the center of your body.

In all three classic strokes you should make contact with the ball in front of you on an imaginary line that is parallel to a vertical line drawn through the center of your body from head to toe. The point of contact on this imaginary line varies with the stroke you are using. In the sidearm and underarm strokes you make contact at a point knee-high or lower; in the overarm stroke you hit the ball at a point level with the top of your head.

Point of contact: not too early,
not too late.

5
Learning
to Stroke

THE WORD "STROKE" has a meaning restricted to the physical grace or action of hitting the ball. You generally practice the strokes alone, so that when you are involved in the vigorous ebb and flow of match play you can use each stroke instinctively in an effort to hit the ball to a selected target. Several drills can help improve your stroking.

DROP-STROKE

The prime purpose of this routine is to provide practice in stroking the moving ball. However, the drop-stroke has career-long value as a warm-up routine. In addition, the drop-stroke is very important in making a good and proper serve. In drop-stroking, the player must decide where he wants the ball to be when he strikes it, a decision that is particularly important when he serves in a game. To put the

41

ball into play under game conditions, the server must step into the service zone, come to a complete stop, then drop the ball and execute a stroke.

For the drop-stroke drill, stand in midcourt on the service line and assume the prestroke stance, then hold the ball in the front hand with your nonstriking arm extended forward and slightly in the direction of the side wall toward which your toes are pointing. The striking arm should be near the position it is in at the conclusion of a backswing.

The hand holding the ball is approximately knee-high, with the back of the hand facing the front wall. Control the ball with your thumb and first finger; you can gain more control by resting the ball on the side of your second finger.

The proper drop.
Hold the ball with the fingers,
not the palm.

Release the ball by moving your hand toward the floor and gently throwing the ball from the tips of thumb and forefinger while bending downward at your waist. Using the fingertips in this way provides some delicate control over the ball, a control that is needed if the ball is to land on the floor and rebound to a specific height (as would be desirable for a serve).

As you release the ball, stride forward on your front foot a comfortable distance and begin the forward swing with

42

your striking arm. This way your hand can strike the ball at the top of the rebound. At this point the ball is almost arrested in space and it is a relatively simple matter to move your hand onto it. All this time, of course, your eyes are

Drop-stroke.
Strike the ball at the height
of the bounce. With practice you can control the height.

focused intently on the moving ball. After practicing for a while, you will begin to see the ball reach the top of the rebound, where you can easily strike it. After your skill increases, try hitting the ball after it leaves this high point and moves toward the floor. Also, try relating the height of your drop to the time necessary for a full backswing to be completed.

43

THROW-STROKE OFF THE FRONT WALL

In this drill the ball moves on a plane more or less horizontal to the floor, rather than up and down with an apparent halt in space as in the drop-stroke. Stroking this ball as it approaches is more difficult than stroking the dropped ball, so you must concentrate fully and at the same time keep your feet moving so that you maintain constant visual contact with the ball.

For the purpose of practice, where the ball goes is not the most important thing, because you have no particular target. Swing easily and save the hard hits until you have more confidence in your ability. If you overswing you will forfeit your form, and good form is one of the keys to good handball. Another primary objective is ambidexterity, so practice with both hands.

SUSTAINED RETURN TO THE FRONT WALL

This drill consists of stroking the ball each time it comes off the front wall, rather than catching it and going into the throw-stroke-off-the-front-wall routine. You will discover how important ball control is, because if you hit the ball too hard or too high, it will rebound off the front wall way out of your reach. In addition to always watching the ball, you must concentrate on how hard you are hitting and where you want the ball to go after it leaves the front wall.

Continue this sustained return routine until the ball is out of play. You may use either hand for striking; in fact, make sure that both hands get some practice. As you try to sustain the pace of this routine, you will be tempted to hit only with your dominant hand.

Count the number of consecutive times you successfully return the ball to the front wall, and move your goal upward as your skill develops—from five to ten to twenty times.

44

This drill also gives you practice in moving from one territory to another, since you will have to adjust your position as the ball comes off the wall at different directions and angles. You will soon discover how essential well-conditioned legs are to good handball.

VOLLEY WITH A FRIEND

Don't bother to serve; simply throw the ball to the front wall while you and another player stand on opposite sides of the court just back of the short line. Try to stroke the ball back to each other, first with one hand, then with the other. At first it will be difficult to control, but after a few practices you can expect to keep the ball in play for several alternate returns. When you have sufficient control to keep the ball in play for a number of returns, you are ready to begin volleying on a competitive basis and to play a game.

6
Tactics

TACTICAL DECISIONS in handball are made primarily to keep your opponent behind center-court territory and moving rapidly. These two tactical goals, which the good veteran player understands well, are highly interrelated but not necessarily identical; that is, you can keep your opponent out of center court but not run him enough to reduce his stamina and accuracy significantly. Tactically, the best sequence of shots is one that forces your opponent not only to stroke the ball from behind center-court territory but also to move swiftly from left to right, right to left, forward and backward.

Tactics, then, require planning or split-second decision making. In a matter of seconds the player must select a target and a stroke, all the while moving his feet constantly so that he can keep the ball always in sight and move within reach of it.

If you spend time in and around handball courts, you will notice that experienced players seldom talk about making a stroke. They almost always talk about a good shot or a missed shot, a kill shot, a pass shot or lob shot. The word "stroke" refers only to the physical action of hitting the ball; the word "shot" implies thinking of a selected target. It also implies a consideration of such variables as the score of the game and positioning of the opponent.

The target is always the place you want the ball ultimately to reach. For instance, the target can be the catcher's glove in baseball, or the inside of a basketball net, or a spot on the floor of a handball court. In baseball, of course, there is only one catcher's glove for the pitcher to focus on, but in handball there are two successive spots on the floor for the ball to reach. It is the second spot that is the target, for the moment the ball touches the floor a second time, the volley is completed.

Most shots exist within the context of a series of shots. Two or more consecutive shots by you and your opponent constitute a series, or volley, as it is termed in handball. The shots of a volley are all interrelated, and an experienced handball player is always thinking ahead to make each shot an effective part of his tactical plan.

THE KILL SHOT

The kill shot, the most enjoyable shot in handball, has only one purpose: to end the volley. For years Jimmy Ja-

A

B

C

Front-wall kill. Try the shot shown in this sequence when your opponent is far behind you. If your opponent is on your right, direct your kill shot to the left, forcing him to try a difficult off-hand shot.

cobs has claimed that you don't go for the kill unless you want to end the volley. The kill is a gutsy shot; the risk is great, but the reward is high. When executed successfully, the kill shot leaves your opponent with no chance to recover and sustain the volley. For that instant you have absolute power over your opponent and the game. The kill is so decisive that even your opponent congratulates you on a shot that leaves him helpless and hopeless.

Sounds tempting, doesn't it? Well, it is, and many players make the mistake of trying a kill shot too often. An unsuccessful kill shot usually produces one of two results: it ends the volley in favor of your opponent, or it gives your opponent a chance for an easy return with which he can gain control of the immediate situation.

The target for all kill shots is a spot on the floor no more than inches away from the front wall. A perfect kill shot is referred to as a rollout, which means that the ball hits so low on the front wall that it actually rebounds onto the floor immediately and rolls on the floor so that it is impossible to play back. It seemingly does not hop up at all.

FRONT-WALL KILL

For this shot, as well as for the back-wall kill and the fly kill, the target is always the same; the best possible kind of shot is a rollout. Thus, these shots are not named on the basis of where you are trying to send the ball; they get their names from the wall from which the ball has just rebounded. For example, when speaking of a front-wall kill the player means that the wall which the ball last touched was the front wall.

The best way to perform the front-wall kill is with a sidearm stroke made as close to the floor as possible. This requires great patience because the player must bend his knees and bend over at the waist as he allows the ball to approach closer and closer to the floor; just before the ball reaches the floor, he begins the forward swing of the side-arm stroke. After the ball is hit it travels, ideally, on a path almost parallel to and only inches above the floor. Such a flight pattern into the front wall is highly preferred, as it almost always results in a rollout.

Theoretically, it does not matter what part of the court your opponent is in at the time you strike the ball, since there is no return for a kill shot. However, such strokes do not always result in a kill; therefore, the beginner should still give some consideration to where his opponent is located. When employing the front-wall kill with the opponent to your left, send the ball to the right half of the frontcourt; with the opponent to your right, send it to the left half. If the opponent is behind you, place the ball so that if he does reach it he must play it with his off hand.

BACK-WALL KILL

The back-wall kill varies from the front-wall kill in that greater distance is involved and more elaborate footwork is required. One of the best opportunities for this shot is when your opponent is also located in the rear portion of the court, for from this location he must start moving forward rapidly if he is to have any chance at all of making a return.

The best way to get into position for a back-wall kill is to follow the ball with your eyes and your feet; as you watch the ball travel toward the back wall, you glide-step toward the back wall. Although the ball will reach the back wall, the player must not, for the ball will rebound off the back wall faster than the player can leave the back wall and move forward. While moving to the rear and watching the ball approach the back wall, you should anticipate where the ball is going to be after it rebounds so that you can stop moving to the rear at a point slightly behind where you predict the rebounding ball would touch the floor. At this spot you reverse direction and glide-step with the ball toward the front wall. As you glide forward, try to time your stroke so that the vertical center-line of your body is opposite the ball when your hand contacts it.

A

Back-wall kill (*above and opposite page*). Glide-step toward the rebound. Step into the ball to make your kill, follow through and move toward center court.

B

C

FLY KILL

The fly kill is the most aggressive shot in handball. As its name implies, you strike the ball on the fly, before it has had time to touch the floor. Many experienced players consider the fly kill the most difficult shot in handball.

The key to this shot is attitude: you must be very aggressive and determined. You must enjoy the faster tempo frequent fly kills introduce into the match. Fly kills, of course, put tremendous pressure on your opponent to be

A

The fly kill (*above and opposite page*). Be aggressive! Don't wait for the ball to hit the floor. Strike it just before it touches. With your opponent on your right, the target is to your left.

B

C

quick and fast. The best chances for achieving a fly kill come when you are no further back from the front wall than center-court territory. It is best to restrict your attempts for a fly kill to returns or serves that are at or below your waist, thus permitting the use of the classic sidearm stroke. It is almost impossible to execute a successful fly kill if the ball is above your waist at the point of contact.

THE PASS SHOT

The pass shot, so named because the ball travels in the air past your opponent on either his left or right side, is the most frequently used shot in handball. It is less risky than the kill shot because the ball need not touch the front wall as close to the floor. When perfectly executed, a pass shot flies past your opponent beyond his reach, thus ending the volley. Less precise passes, however, can be helpful. A hard, fast-moving pass may force your opponent out of center court, thus opening the way for you to occupy this much desired territory. Finally, your pass shots may simply keep your opponent running, which is one of the most important tactical considerations.

Since the pass shot is so frequently used, most points are earned from the pass. Therefore, you should practice this shot more than any other.

The target for the pass shot is always a point in the back of the court that, you hope, is impossible for your opponent to reach while the ball is in play. One of the most common passes is a fast-moving ball that travels close to and parallel with one of the side walls (see Alley Pass, page 57). Such a pass, at the least, forces your opponent to stroke the ball while outside center-court territory. Another type of pass shot is one that rebounds off the front wall and, before reaching the floor, touches a side wall at a point perpendicular to your opponent's territorial location (see Angle Pass, page 58). Such a flight pattern makes the ball come off the side wall in a path almost directly opposite to the path in which an inexperienced opponent is likely to be moving, thus forcing him to pivot before chasing the ball into the backcourt area.

ALLEY PASS

From a tactical viewpoint, pass shots are both offensive and defensive. Because of this dual purpose, they are used more frequently than kills, which are offensive, and lobs, which are defensive. The alley pass is designed to travel

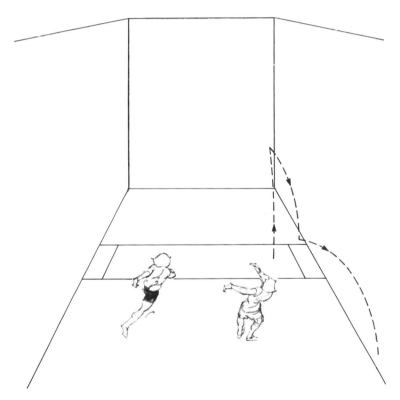

The alley pass. Take advantage of your opponent's being on the opposite side of the court.

close to a side wall but not to touch it. A tactically sound time to go for the alley pass is when your opponent is on the opposite side of the court from you, for he must run a great distance to reach this shot from there, and, even if he does reach it, he has been forced into backcourt territory.

ANGLE PASS

The angle pass is a good shot to use when your opponent is occupying center-court territory; it is particularly helpful if your opponent is a poor judge of side-wall rebounds. In this shot the ball should, before it touches the floor, rebound off the front wall and into a side wall at a point

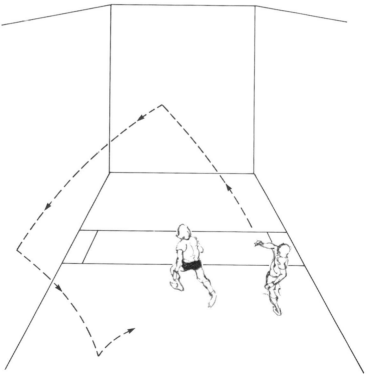

The angle pass. Force your opponent to make an awkward pivot.

perpendicular to your opponent's location. Ideally, the ball will come off the side wall in the opposite direction from the one in which your opponent has started to move after incorrectly anticipating the rebound off the side wall. This forces him to pivot (a difficult maneuver) in order to chase the ball into the backcourt area.

CROSSCOURT PASS

The crosscourt pass is a shot that is directed at one of the back-wall corners. You use it when your opponent is out of center-court territory; for example, when you and he are both positioned right of center court, you could send a crosscourt pass into the back left corner.

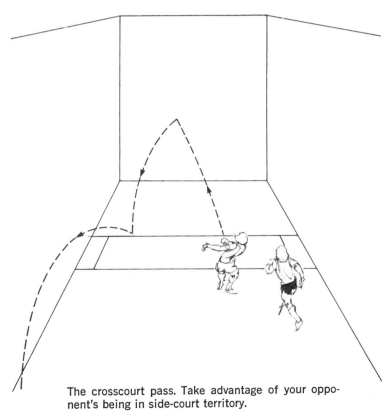

The crosscourt pass. Take advantage of your opponent's being in side-court territory.

Like the alley and angle passes, the crosscourt pass can be performed with any of the classic strokes and with either hand. Which hand and which stroke to use at a given moment in a match depends on the game situation and the skill you have developed through practice and experience.

THE LOB SHOT

The lob shot characteristically travels more slowly and in a higher arc than do the kill and pass shots. The strength of the lob is the subtle nature of its movement; it is not a power shot. Many veteran players consider the lob modern-day handball's most sophisticated shot.

The target for the lob shot is always a spot on the floor in backcourt territory that is close to one of the side walls and back wall, because this is where a slow-moving ball is most difficult to hit. The closer the shot is to a corner, the less room your opponent has to stroke the ball.

Experienced players use the slower-moving lob in order to change the tempo of a volley. By thus slowing the action, the player gets a chance to rest a little from the fast and furious pace of the game. He can also use this time to think about the opponent and the game situation. Furthermore, the change in tempo forces his opponent to adjust to the ball's reduced speed, a difficult task in itself. For example, the slower-moving ball may prove frustrating to an opponent who prefers to move quickly and strongly into his next stroke; like the good fast ball hitter in baseball, this type of player has great difficulty in waiting for a slower ball to arrive.

You can use the lob shot to force your opponent into backcourt territory. For example, if he is overpowering you with his kills and passes, you have little to lose by forcing him into backcourt territory. Forcing him to the rear increases the distance his shots must travel, thereby reducing his accuracy. If your opponent proves to be an excellent shot maker from the backcourt area, you will probably lose the game—but at least you have made it more difficult for him to win. However, if he proves to be ineffective from the backcourt, your chances of winning are vastly improved.

STRAIGHT LOB

Lob shots, unlike kill shots, are primarily defensive in nature; that is to say, you would use a lob most often when your opponent has the upper hand. In the case of the straight lob, which may be executed with any of the three classic strokes, the objective is to have the ball move straight into the top half of the front wall, return in a pathway close to one of the side walls, then fall to the floor about midcourt and rebound high into the air without reaching the back wall (see illustration on page 69). Such a flight pattern forces your opponent to stroke the ball as it moves almost perpendicular to the floor, which is very difficult to do with accuracy, especially when the ball is also close to a side wall. This shot may be useful in slowing down a very aggressive opponent; it may also be used to advantage against an opponent with a weak or ineffective overhand stroke.

CROSSCOURT LOB

The crosscourt lob, like the straight lob, can be performed with either the sidearm, underarm or overarm stroke. In this shot your return touches a side wall, then the front wall and finally the other side wall before touching the floor at about three-quarter court and rebounding to the first side wall. The tactical goal in this shot is to force your opponent to stroke the ball as it approaches from an unusual angle, in the hope of catching him for an instant somewhat unprepared. It is chiefly the element of surprise that makes this shot effective, since your opponent will have to move very fast in order to get to a ball that is approaching suddenly from an unexpected angle. The crosscourt lob can be very helpful when you are confronted with a difficult try—for example, when the opponent has delivered a carefully placed low, hard serve to your off hand.

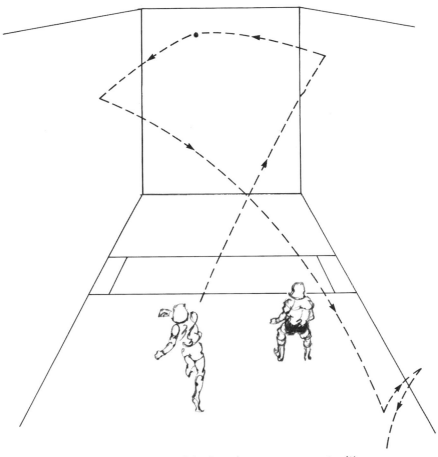

The crosscourt lob. Surprise your opponent with a shot from wall to wall to wall.

CEILING LOB

The ceiling lob is usually performed with the classical overhand stroke, although it can also be performed well with an underhand stroke. The target is a spot on the floor only a few inches from one of the two back corners of the court. In this shot you hit a softly moving ball that eventually rebounds off the floor at or near the front line in a high arc above your opponent's head, travels to and gently touches the back wall, then drops almost vertically to the floor within a few inches of both the back wall and one of the side walls (that is, near a rear corner). The ball

The ceiling lob. Excellent for forcing your opponent back and into the corners.

can reach this target regardless of whether it hits the ceiling and then the front wall, or the front wall and then the ceiling.

Beginners should practice the front-wall-then-ceiling shot only from in front of the short line. Even sophisticated players seldom attempt this shot from behind the short line. The ceiling lob, in either case, can buy time for you while it travels slowly about the court. Paul Haber has been known upon occasion to have the ceiling lob under such great control that it could be used offensively rather than defensively, but such skill is most rare.

The serve is a relatively leisurely shot. Before serving, be aware of where your opponent is located and try to conceal where you are

THE SERVE

The serve is a shot, not a stroke. It is correctly described as the most leisurely shot in handball because you have ten seconds in which to execute it. (For no other shot do you have this much time.) You have time to think about your target, your starting location and the stroke you are going to use. During this allotted period the whole zone between the front line and the short line, from side wall to side wall (see Diagram 3 in Chapter 1), is legally your territory and the opponent is forbidden to enter.

planning to aim the ball. As soon as you have followed through, step back to center-court territory.

To receive a serve, a receiver must stand at least 5 feet behind the short line and remain at least this far away from the short line until after the server's hand strikes the ball. This does not mean, however, that the receiver must stand still while the server drops the ball and executes his stroke; the rules permit the receiver to stand or move about, as long as he does not get within 5 feet of the short line. Unlike the server, who must come to a complete stop inside the service area before initiating the drop-stroke, the receiver may move constantly. (The receiver may also move in order to distract the server.) As soon as the server's hand strikes the ball, the receiver may move forward as far as the short line without penalty; to avoid a penalty, however, all parts of the receiver's body, including the striking hand, must be behind the short line not only when the ball is hit but also at the completion of the follow-through.

When it is your turn to serve, walk to a location that provides the best chance for you to successfully execute the type of serve you have decided to try. If you wish, you can start from the same spot time and time again, or vary your starting location with each serve. However, you "must serve off one bounce." This official rule, seemingly straightforward, nonetheless has a particular tactical possibility. It means that you must drop the ball and strike it before it touches the floor a second time unless you catch the ball with the hand that dropped it to the floor. Thus, the receiver has more difficulty in anticipating the timing of your serve. You are allowed only two drop-and-catch opportunities for each service attempt; on the third drop you must stroke the ball if you are to avoid an out.

The target for the serve is any one of an infinite number of spots on the back half of the floor. The target you choose should give you an immediate advantage, especially if it is your first service attempt. (You are allowed another attempt if the first attempt is judged short or long.) As in tennis, the ultimate serve is an ace.

LOW, HARD SERVE

The primary purpose of the low, hard serve is to force your opponent outside center-court territory and into the back-wall area. In addition, however, the low, hard serve can be an ace. Many experienced players try for an ace on the first serve of the two attempts allowed by the rules. A third purpose of the low, hard serve is to force your opponent into moving quickly without much time for thinking about his footwork.

You can practice the low, hard serve from different locations in the service zone. It is probably best to start off in

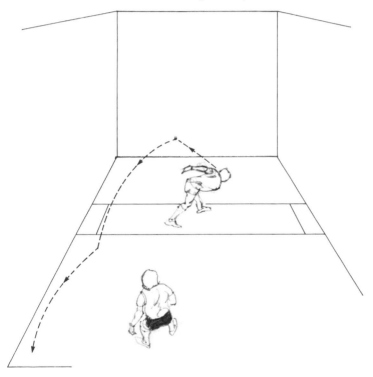

The low, hard serve.
Force your opponent to move for the ball.

the center of the service territory and, using your dominant hand, practice serving the ball into one of the rear portions of the back-wall area. From the beginning, however, you should direct a few low, hard serves at other rear portions of the court, for your goal is to be able to propel the ball to a number of possible targets. While practicing, keep your eye on the ball as it approaches the front wall and notice how high off the floor the ball touches this surface. Your serve should not reach the front wall either too close to or too far from the floor. Remember that from the front wall your serve must travel a minimum of 20 feet in the air in order to pass over the short line. Remember, too, that a serve can be too long; that is, if it hits the back wall before touching the floor, it is illegal and must, according to the rules, be classified the same as a short.

LOB SERVE

The lob serve, like the low, hard serve, is meant to force your opponent away from center court and into the back-wall area. In addition, it should force him to execute an overarm stroke with his off hand to return the ball. An overarm stroke from the back-wall area is a relatively difficult task for most players, particularly for beginners. Even if your opponent makes a successful return, it is very likely to be one that gives you the advantage.

You can initiate the lob serve from any point in the service zone, and you can use any of the classical strokes. The ball should touch the front wall fairly high so that after it leaves the front wall it will travel high and slowly toward the front line and eventually drop almost vertically onto a point slightly behind the short line. The ball will rebound high into the air and will most likely force your opponent to use an overarm stroke.

68

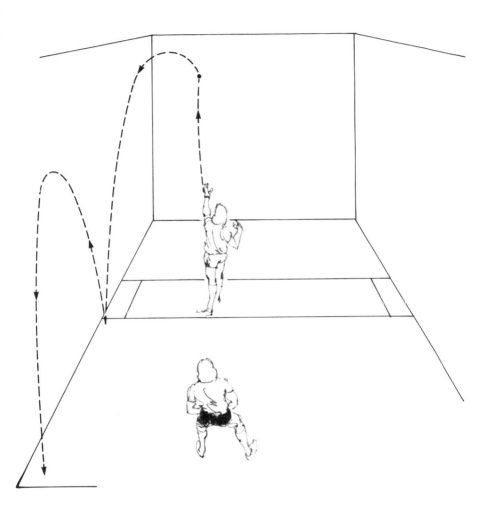

The lob serve.
Keep your opponent in backcourt territory.

OFF-HAND FORCE SERVE

The primary purpose of the off-hand force is to require your opponent to execute the return with his off hand, the one he uses less and certainly does not prefer to use. (This serve is sometimes called the Scotch-toss, three-wall or Z-serve.)

Initially, you should practice the off-hand force only from the extreme left or extreme right of the service area. Since the left hand will be the off hand of most of your opponents, you need more practice serving from the extreme

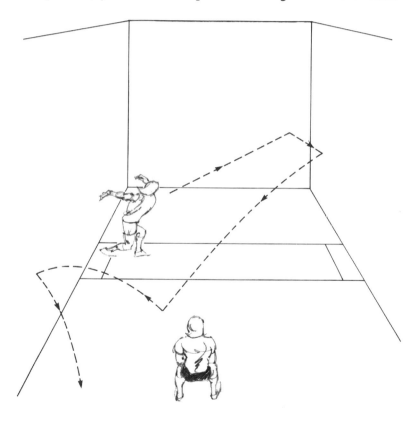

Off-hand force serve.
Force your opponent to use his off hand.

left of the service zone than from the extreme right. The heel of your rear foot should be only 2 or 3 inches from the side wall when you are in the starting position.

Although you may use any of the classic strokes, the best way to practice the off-hand force initially is to use the same stroke you use for the low, hard serve. After stroking the ball, watch it approach the front wall and note how high off the floor the ball touches this surface. Also note how close to the extreme right edge of the front wall your serve is placed; the closer to the right edge of the front wall you can send the ball, the closer to the front wall the serve will touch the side wall. The planned path of the ball is front wall, side wall, floor, and then the other side wall. The target is any portion of the floor located near your opponent's off hand. Your tactical goal is the same as for the crosscourt lob: to force your opponent to stroke the ball as it arrives at a difficult angle.

DELIBERATE SIDE-WALL PLAY

Beginning handball players understandably concentrate their attention on the front wall; after all, each serve and each return must legally reach the front wall in order not to end the point. The experienced player, however, may deliberately use the side walls to gain advantages and win volleys, for he knows that many shots can be more effective if the ball rebounds from one or more of the side walls.

Beginning players are actually surprised by some of the rebounds off the side walls. This is to be expected, as most ball games do not provide experience with side walls. The best way to become familiar with side-wall rebounds is to practice hitting off the side wall. One way to do this is to introduce a rule into games between beginners: each serve or return must touch at least one side wall either before or after it hits the front wall; a serve or return that fails to do so results in an out.

DELIBERATE BALL SPIN

Although experienced handball players deliberately apply spin to the ball, they very seldom use the word "spin." Rather, they use such terms as "natural," "reverse" and "hook." The terms "natural" and "reverse" refer to the action of the forearm and hand, not the direction in which the ball bounces after it has touched the floor. It is a "natural" function of the flexion-extension motion in the sidearm or underarm stroke to begin turning the palm of the hand away from the body as you contact the ball; the "reverse" of this action is when a player turns the palm toward his body.

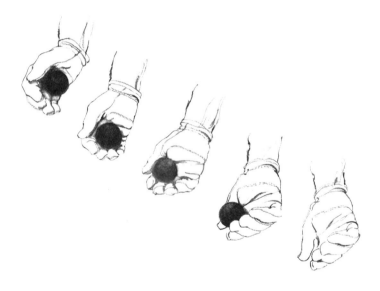

Natural spin. Undercut the ball.

A hook is merely a general term that refers to either a natural or a reverse. For a right-hander who has just stroked a shot that goes directly from his dominant hand to the front wall and then to the floor, a natural is a return that hooks to the left after touching the floor; under the same circumstances, a reverse is a shot that hooks to the right.

Once you are able to use both types of hooks deliberately, you can surprise your opponent if he begins anticipating too far in advance. By executing one type of hook all the time, of course, you make it easy for your opponent to

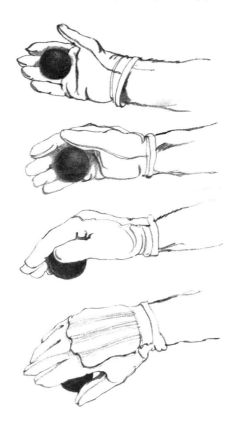

Reverse spin. Roll the hand over the ball.

anticipate correctly; but once he knows that you can deliver both types, he must be more cautious about taking that extra helpful step ahead of time. In other words, you "keep him honest."

PLAYING THE PERCENTAGES

As in baseball, "playing the percentages" is a part of handball. Veteran handball players try to execute the action that succeeds the most frequently of possible actions. For example, experienced handball players know that the best chance of success with a kill shot comes when the shooter is located on or in front of the short line. Knowing this does not prevent the player from trying a kill shot from rear court, but it does reduce the number of times he attempts such a kill, for the percentages are against him, not with him, on a kill attempt from rear court.

Playing the percentages, however, despite the easy example just given, is a complicated art and requires years of experience and thinking to master. Innumerable variables can influence the percentages: the game score, the match score, your own skills, your opponent's skills, the respective locations of the players, fatigue, etc. You must account for all the possibilities and their interrelationships. This is a difficult—almost an impossible—task, but the time to begin is now.

7
Practicing
the Shots

PRACTICE may not make perfect, as is so frequently claimed, but it certainly is the road toward becoming a skilled handball player. We have selected a number of drills that are helpful for beginners. Throughout these drills or practice routines you should work on improving your classical stroking.

We recommend practicing the pass shot first and foremost, since this shot does not require the precision of the kill and is less sophisticated than the lob shot. With the pass shot you keep the ball in play with relative ease, which allows you to practice volleying with another player or to play a game.

DRILL NUMBER 1

This drill is designed to improve your pass shot. During this drill you stroke from nine different locations, all of which are shown in the accompanying diagram. The drill begins

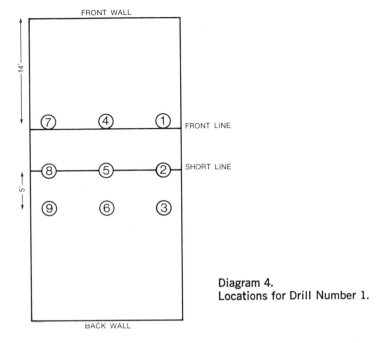

FRONT WALL

14'

⑦   ④   ① FRONT LINE

⑧   ⑤   ② SHORT LINE

5'

⑨   ⑥   ③

Diagram 4.
Locations for Drill Number 1.

BACK WALL

from location number 1, which is less than 15 feet from the front wall. Place your feet just forward of the front line, with toes pointed toward the right wall. With the right hand, make an easy underhand toss toward the front wall; the ball should hit the front wall first, then bounce softly back toward you. Let the ball bounce toward you after hitting the floor; as it comes within range, glide forward with your feet and execute the classic sidearm stroke. Your objective is to have the ball hit the front wall and rebound back between you and the right wall. What you aim for is a flight path that is parallel to and within a few inches of the right wall. As the ball passes you, turn your head and watch it as it goes into the backcourt area. By watching the ball, you will begin to know what target such shots eventually reach.

After three tries from location number 1, move to location number 2 and repeat the three tries. Then move to spot number 3 and repeat. From location number 4, make six attempts, the first three with the right hand, the second three with the left hand. Remember that when you use your left hand for striking, your toes are initially pointed toward the left wall. Now move to spot number 5 and execute six more passes with the sidearm stroke. Your objective is simple: to achieve a pass shot whose flight path is parallel to and somewhat close to the appropriate side wall.

After using both hands when you stroke from location number 6, move to spot 7 and practice with your left hand. After three attempts to return the ball parallel to and very close to the left wall, move to spots 8 and 9 and repeat this procedure, always using the sidearm stroke.

DRILL NUMBER 2

The purpose of this drill is to improve your lob shots. Performed from the backcourt area, it is designed to teach

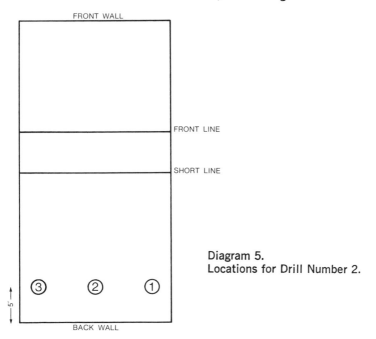

Diagram 5.
Locations for Drill Number 2.

you how to keep the ball in play from this territory, which is a long distance from the front wall. In this drill you stroke from the three different locations shown in the diagram. Note that all these spots are 5 feet in front of the back wall.

At location 1, point your toes toward the right wall. Using your right hand, throw the ball with an overhand motion to the front wall so that the ball returns high and slowly on the fly to a spot just behind the short line. The ball will then rebound high and toward you. Adjust yourself to each return so you can execute an overarm stroke; your objective is to send the ball back to the top area of the front wall in a high arching trajectory so that it next touches the floor just behind the short line and then rebounds high into the backcourt area.

Obviously, a good throw and a good overarm shot in this drill will bring the ball back to your starting location time and time again. However, we recommend that initially you catch each of these practice shots and hold the ball just before it reaches the floor following the rebound from near the short line. By catching and holding the ball at this location, you see where you are and where indeed the ball did reach; you can also recall where this practice shot hit the front wall and where it first touched the floor.

After three attempts, move to location number 2 and make these attempts with the right hand and then with the left. Next, move to spot 3 and use your left hand the same number of times. These practice attempts, totaling twelve from the backcourt area, can be worked into your warm-up routine very easily. All these drills require only a few minutes to complete.

DRILL NUMBER 3

This drill is designed to improve your kill shot. (For locations, see the diagram.) It begins from location num-

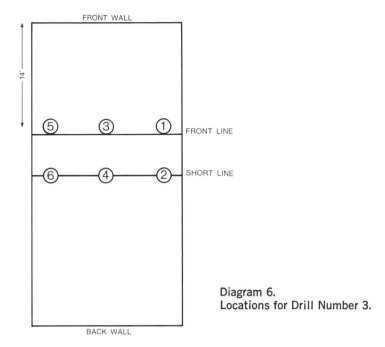

FRONT WALL

14'

⑤   ③   ① FRONT LINE

⑥———④———② SHORT LINE

Diagram 6.
Locations for Drill Number 3.

BACK WALL

ber 1, which is no more than 14 feet from the front wall. Place your right foot slightly forward of the front line, with your toes pointed toward the right wall. This forces your left foot to be a step ahead of the front line. With your right hand, make an easy underhand toss toward the front wall; you want the ball to return short of where you are so that you are forced to stride forward to stroke the ball before it hits the floor a second time. A soft toss that touches the front wall at a point approximately 5 feet above the floor usually produces a return that is knee-high or lower when you stroke it. Ideally, your stroke is made when the ball is only inches above the floor, as this allows you, using the sidearm stroke, to propel it with full power into the front wall an inch or two above the floor. You will have to bend your knees considerably to hit this low ball; in addition, you will have to bend your body forward from the

79

waist and spread your feet farther apart than usual. After three attempts, move to location number 2 and, with your right foot on the short line, try three more kill shots with your right hand.

Next, move to location 3 and with your right hand make three more kill shots. Then try three times with your left hand. Remember that when you use your left hand in this drill, your left foot should be slightly forward of the front line and your right foot should be a whole step ahead. The toes of both feet are pointed toward the left wall.

Now do the drill three times with each hand from locations 4, 5 and 6. Watch where your shot goes. How low does it hit the front wall? Remember that your objective is to have the ball move from the front wall to a spot on the floor just inches from the front wall, from which location it will roll along the floor and leave your opponent feeling helpless and hopeless.

8
Attacking
Your Opponent

IN THE FIRST FEW WEEKS of your handball career, you will be primarily concerned with keeping the ball in play. However, as your skill increases, you will start wanting to win instead of simply volleying with a friend. You should now ask yourself: What do I know about my opponent?

If you have played against your opponent or observed his play in contests with others, you probably have some information about his strengths and weaknesses. If you have never played against him before, ask other handball players who have played him what they know. It is quite ethical to investigate your opponent in this way; you can be sure that if he is an experienced player, he is developing a scouting report on you! It is foolish not to ask the same questions about him: what are his natural talents (for instance, is he a righty or a lefty?); what style characterizes his play (is he a killer, a passer or a softer?).

THE KILLER

A killer is a player who likes to shoot often. He deliberately positions himself for opportunities to go for the kill or bottom-board rollout shot. Usually this is his best shot, so he enjoys employing it and does so frequently.

The killer is an impatient player who likes to end the volley as soon as possible. In fact, he is so anxious to end the volley that he often goes for the kill even though the odds for success are against him. He has his best chance for success when he is positioned on or in front of the short line, less than 20 feet from the front wall. If your opponent is a killer, you can use this knowledge to reduce his effective-

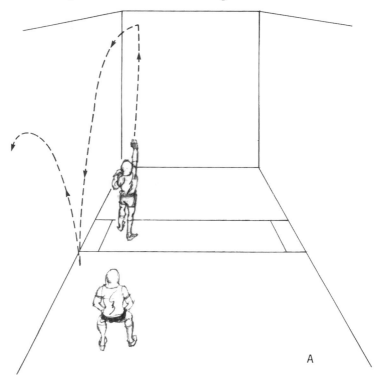

Serving to a killer. Try to keep a killer away from center court by using a lob serve (A). This forces him into the corner to make

ness by placing your returns in the backcourt. Remember, however, that the killer will take a chance on the kill shot from any location. Keeping the ball in backcourt does not eliminate kill-shot attempts, but it does greatly reduce the odds for success.

SERVING TO A KILLER

The best serve to use against a killer is the lob serve. Since a killer is aggressive and dislikes waiting for the slower-moving ball, you should place yourself within the service

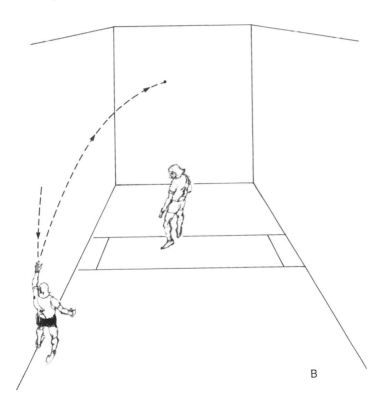

an overhand shot and allows you to take the favored center-court position (B).

box very close to the side wall that corresponds to your opponent's off hand. Next, drop the ball for an overarm stroke and hit it in a soft arc so that it touches the front wall very close to the top and very close to the side wall nearest you. This serve should touch the floor just beyond the short line and near the side wall that corresponds to your opponent's off hand, from which position it will bounce in a high trajectory toward the backcourt and remain close to the side wall. Such a serve requires both skill and patience to return; even if your opponent has the skill, he may not have the patience. You, of course, have moved from the service box to center-court territory while the ball has been traveling to the front wall and into the backcourt area. Since you are competing with a killer, you should expect him to try for a kill; therefore, it is wise to position yourself along the front edge of center-court territory, where you are a step closer to his likely target.

If your serve is well placed, the killer may be forced to counter with a lob shot of his own. Assuming that his return lob keeps the ball in play, what do you do? The best strategy is to counter with another lob, for once you have a killer engaged in a lob sequence, you want to keep him there. Remember, the tempo of the lob game is not to his liking, nor are his skills as highly developed in this style of play. Let him make the first mistake.

There are two kinds of mistakes a killer can make: (1) his return fails to reach the front wall, which means that you win the volley; (2) his return keeps the ball in play but leaves you with a setup or easy kill opportunity. When this happens, you must have the courage to move in aggressively and attempt to end the volley with a kill shot of your own.

THE PASSER

This type of player likes to hit the ball hard. He usually hits the ball hard regardless of where he is on the court, and his shots usually carom around the court from wall to wall or speed parallel to one of the side walls. On rare occasions, the passer will also direct a very hard shot to the ceiling; this powerful shot is a rather sure sign that the player is indeed a passer, for a person with greater control over his skills and feelings will use a lob shot to the ceiling rather than a powerfully hit, fast-moving ball.

The passer bases his strategy on a fast-moving ball that gives his opponent very little time to set himself for the return. He is very much like the killer in that he is aggressive. The passer is basically getting his fun from the physical sensation of hitting the ball hard and overpowering his opponent.

SERVING TO A PASSER

There are more passers in handball than killers or softers, which is not surprising because the pass shot is less risky than the kill shot, the physical sensation of hitting the ball hard is satisfying and the psychological satisfaction of overpowering your opponent is enormous. Until you can classify an opponent definitely as a killer or a softer, assume that he is a passer.

The best serve to use against a passer is the low, hard serve. For this shot, stand in the center of the service box and drop the ball for a sidearm stroke. If the passer's off hand is his left, you want your service to strike the front wall just to the left of center and, of course, not very high from the floor. The ball should bounce off the front wall in a fairly flat trajectory and travel toward the left rear corner of the court. Your target is a spot on the floor just in front of the back wall. As your serve travels toward this spot, quickly move into center-court territory. Since your opponent is a passer, position yourself at the rear edge of center-court territory. By being in this portion of center court (rather than the front part, as is the case when playing a killer), you give yourself more time to intercept the passer's expected pass shot.

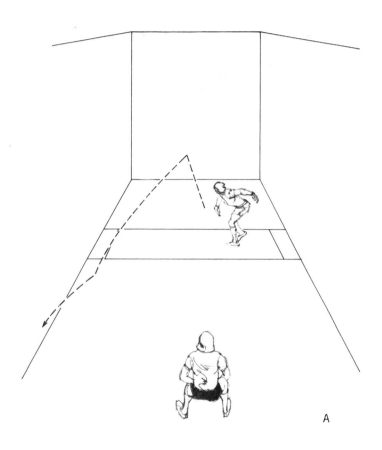

A

Serving to a passer. Use a low, hard serve to his off hand (A) and be prepared to move to center court, where you have territorial advantage (B).

A well-placed low, hard serve forces the passer to move quickly after it and swing upward at the ball, which is not easy. Most likely, the passer will make a successful return of a low, hard serve with his fist, and the ball will travel in a high trajectory to the front wall. Having forced the passer to hit a lob shot, you now want to keep the volley alive with another lob. If you can do this, chances are that the passer will lose his patience with this slow tempo and will make the first mistake. What you want him to do is either fail to make his return reach the front wall or leave you with an easy kill opportunity.

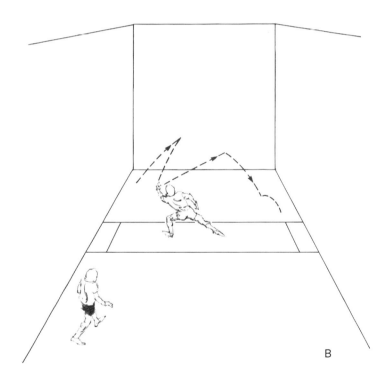

B

THE SOFTER

The strategy of the softer, compared to that of the killer and passer, is to keep the game at a slower tempo. This relative slowness is ill-suited to strong young killers and passers, who prefer to move quickly and furiously into the next stroke, and the softer seeks to frustrate such opponents by forcing them to exert their natural aggressiveness against slower-moving returns. What the softer desires most is to have his opponent accept this slower pace and use the lob game himself, for unless the opponent is an experienced player, he is almost assuredly doomed to defeat once he elects to play the softer's favorite style. The experienced softer will keep his opponent in the backcourt area while he himself controls center-court territory.

SERVING TO A SOFTER

If your opponent returns the ball time and time again with lob shots, you are up against a softer. Since many players consider the lob to be handball's most sophisticated shot, it is clear that an opponent who is skillful enough to build his style on the various lobs is, more or less by definition, a sophisticated player. If he is an older man who began playing at a young age, when faster tempos were comfortable for him, you can expect him to play wisely with delicate, skillful shots.

The best attack against a softer is to hit fast-moving shots that force him to chase after them. The softer likes to strike a slow-moving ball, so you force him to hit a swiftly moving one. The softer likes to glide-step slowly about the court, so you make him move quickly in order to reach each of your shots.

A good way to begin is by executing an off-hand force serve. For this serve, assuming that the softer's off hand is his left, locate yourself at the extreme left edge of the

88

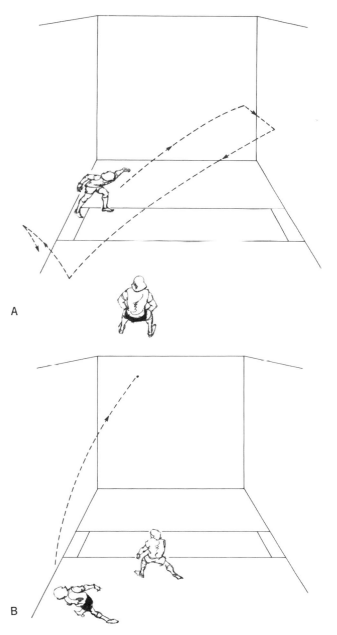

A

B

Serving to a softer. Deliver an off-hand force serve to make him move for the ball (A). You can control center-court territory as he reaches for your serve (B).

service box. Drop the ball for a sidearm stroke. The serve should touch the front wall at a spot close to the right wall and somewhat close to the floor. You want the ball to travel from your hand to the front wall, then to the right wall, then to a point on the floor behind the short line, then to the left wall, and then to the floor again. While the ball is traveling along this complicated pathway toward your selected target, you are moving from the extreme left edge of the service box to the center point of center-court territory. From this location you can either move forward for a fly kill, if the softer's return lob is weak and sets you up for this, or move to the rear if his return lob is skillfully executed and forces you to play your next shot from the backcourt area.

You want to force the softer to return this serve with his off hand while he is pivoting quickly, because in executing such a difficult maneuver he will probably make the first mistake of the volley. Such a mistake, at best, leaves the softer on the defensive, and it may result in an immediate opportunity for you to win the point with a kill shot.

WINNING THE RIGHT TO SERVE

At the beginning of a game you can toss a coin to decide who has the opportunity to serve first. However, few, if any, handballers arrive in the court with a coin, so most players use a more popular procedure called "tossing for the short line," in which the players are positioned near the back wall and each one takes a turn throwing the game ball directly to the front wall; the winner is the person whose throw bounces off the front wall and first touches the floor closest to the short line. Since having the first opportunity at service can be a distinct advantage, you should practice tossing for the short line during your warm-up period.

90

There are also three other methods of deciding who serves first: (1) the older player is awarded this opportunity in recognition of his seniority (this particular method is not recommended unless you are certain you are older than your opponent); (2) the loser of the last game is permitted to serve first, or a player may offer the first service to an opponent whom, in recent months, he has regularly defeated; (3) the owner of the game ball is allowed to serve first (experienced players have been known to appear in the court with a newly purchased ball in order to guarantee that they get the coveted first service).

Once the game is under way, the only means of winning the right to serve is to win a volley that your opponent begins from the service box. If you are the receiver, the odds are against you, for it is the server who holds the initiative: he has ten seconds to select a target, he initiates play and he has a better court location. This is a tough situation for the receiver, particularly a beginning player, so it is best for him to hit a lob shot. If successful, the lob (the percentage shot for a beginner in this situation) will force the server out of center-court position and give the receiver an opportunity to regain the initiative.

MOVING AFTER THE SERVE

No matter whether you are serving to a killer, a passer or a softer; no matter what the score is; no matter which serve you elect to use; no matter what target you have selected—in short, no matter what—you move into center-court territory as soon as your serve is on its way. Don't wait; move immediately! Center court is a priceless piece of real estate, and much too valuable to leave to your opponent. To win at handball you must constantly try for possession of this area, and as server you have an excellent chance to occupy this territory. You should aim your serve in such a way that your opponent is forced to stroke the ball while outside center court, thus leaving it available to you. The worst possible serve is one that allows your opponent to stroke the ball while in possession of center-court territory.

ATTACKING WITH BOTH HANDS

In handball there is no substitute for ambidexterity. Superior speed, strength, youthfulness, intelligence, and all other attributes are singly and collectively inadequate if you do not develop skill with your off hand in conjunction with your dominant hand. Winning points in handball requires a high degree of equality between your two hands. Fortunately, ambidexterity *can* be learned; probably few, if any, handball veterans started out their careers ambidextrous.

Attacking with the off hand may cost you a few points at the beginning of your handball career, but it will pay off later. The inclination among beginners is to rely more on those newly acquired skills that prove successful in competition, which are invariably strong-hand skills. Unfortunately, if you rely wholly on your dominant-hand skills, you will develop a highly specialized set of shots that are successful only when your opponent is not skillful enough to place the ball where you are vulnerable. You can expect a sophisticated player to take advantage of one-sidedness as soon as he discovers that you have failed to develop ambidexterity. And don't expect any mercy—handball players play to win!

Glossary

ACE. A legal serve that the opponent cannot reach with either hand. It earns one point for the server.

ATTEMPTED RETURN. A ball already in play that is hit but fails to reach the front wall legally. Such a ball is out-of-play, and the player hitting it is penalized either by loss of service or by assigning one point to the other player.

CENTER-COURT TERRITORY. An imaginary circular area on the floor near the center of the court just behind the short line. It is approximately 6 feet in diameter. (See Diagram 2 in Chapter 1.)

CROTCH BALL. A ball that seemingly strikes two of the court's playing surfaces simultaneously—for example, the front wall and a side wall, or the floor and the back wall. Whenever the floor is involved, it is always assumed that the ball touched the floor first.

CUTTHROAT. Handball played by three players, with the server playing against the other two. Local rules dictate the methodology of rotating servers and serves; when you are invited to play, it is best simply to ask the local rules of cutthroat.

DIG. A successful return of an opponent's shot that has rebounded in a flat trajectory from a spot very low on the front wall.

DOUBLES. Handball played by four players, two on each side.

FIST BALL. A return or a serve made by striking the ball with the back of the fingers while the fingers are closed tightly onto the heel of the hand. (See illustration on page 22.) Such contact with the ball is legal.

GET. A successful return of an extremely difficult shot.

HINDER. Interference with an opponent's attempt to return the ball legally to the front wall. The opponent must be given unobstructed vision of and access to the ball.

HOOK. A ball that, after touching the front wall, lands on the floor and rebounds either to the left or right of a straight-line pathway.

KILL. A shot that hits the front wall an inch or so above the floor and immediately rolls across the floor. It seemingly does not hop up at all, so the opponent cannot return it.

LONG. A serve that fails to touch the floor behind the short line before touching the back wall. Such a serve is illegal.

OFF HAND. The hand opposite to the player's dominant hand.

ONE-WALL HANDBALL. Handball played in a court that consists only of a front wall and a floor.

POINT OF CONTACT. The point in space where a player's hand meets the ball.

ROLLOUT. The ultimate in kill shots, where the ball hits so low on the front wall that it rebounds onto the floor and rolls so that it is impossible to play back.

SHOOT. To attempt a kill.

SHORT LINE. See Diagram 3 in Chapter 1.

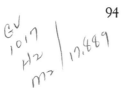
CAMROSE LUTHERAN COLLEGE
LIBRARY

SINGLES. Handball played by two players, one on each team.

STRADDLE BALL. A ball that travels between the legs of a player without touching the player. Such an act may or may not be ruled a hinder.

THREE-WALL HANDBALL. Handball played in a court that consists of a front wall, a floor, and two side walls.

VOLLEY. An exchange of two or more shots. (In badminton, squash and tennis this type of exchange is called a rally.)

WRIST BALL. A ball that touches any part of the wrist. Such contact with the ball is illegal.